# COMFORT and DEVOTION

## A Quilting Tribute to Nurses of the Civil War

### By SARAH MAXWELL and DOLORES SMITH

# COMFORT and DEVOTION

## A Quilting Tribute to Nurses of the Civil War
### By SARAH MAXWELL and DOLORES SMITH

Editor: Kimber Mitchell
Designer: Bob Deck
Photography: Aaron T. Leimkuehler
Illustration: Lon Eric Craven
Technical Editor: Deanna Hodson
Photo Editor: Jo Ann Groves

Published by:
Kansas City Star Books
1729 Grand Blvd.
Kansas City, Missouri, USA 64108

First edition, first printing
ISBN: 978-1-61169-099-6

Library of Congress Control Number: 2013944276

Printed in the United States of America by Walsworth Publishing Co., Marceline, MO

To order copies, call StarInfo at (816) 234-4242.

# COMFORT and DEVOTION

## A Quilting Tribute to Nurses of the Civil War

### By SARAH MAXWELL and DOLORES SMITH

# ABOUT *the* AUTHORS

Sarah Maxwell (right) and Dolores Smith (left) have owned Homestead Hearth in Mexico, Missouri, since September 2002. Their love of history is reflected in the numerous reproduction fabrics showcased in their shop and in the quilts they design. Sarah and Dolores' work is regularly featured in numerous quilt magazines and as free projects for fabric companies. This is their fourth book with Kansas City Star Quilts. Sarah and her husband, Joe, live in Mexico and have two daughters, Megan and Shannen. Dolores and her husband, Brian, have two sons, Ryan and Kyle, and will soon welcome a daughter-in-law, Dharti.

# TABLE *of* CONTENTS

Dedication ............................................................. 6

Acknowledgments ............................................... 7

Introduction ....................................................... 8

General Instructions ........................................ 10

Dorothea Dix ...................................................... 11

Metro Baskets ................................................... 13

Clara Barton ...................................................... 18

Red Cross ........................................................... 21

Eliza Gillespie ................................................... 28

Riding the Rails ................................................ 29

Mary Ann Bickerdyke ..................................... 33

New Nation ........................................................ 35

Hannah Ropes .................................................... 41

Squared Up ........................................................ 43

Jane Newton Woolsey ...................................... 47

Hot Cross Buns ................................................. 48

Kate Cumming ................................................... 55

Fields of Greens ............................................... 56

Cornelia Hancock .............................................. 66

The Blue and the Gray ..................................... 68

Mary Phinney ..................................................... 74

Old Glory ............................................................ 76

# DEDICATION

**SARAH MAXWELL**
As I've worked on *Comfort and Devotion* over the last two years, I've watched my daughters mature into exceptional young women. With Megan about to finish a master's degree and Shannen about to embark on her collegiate career, I am continually impressed by their accomplishments and their dedication to making the world a better place. The nurses profiled in this book made it possible for today's young women to have meaningful careers. This book is dedicated to Megan and Shannen and to young women everywhere who have a world of opportunities, thanks to the women from the past who overcame so many obstacles. Thanks, girls, for putting up with Mom's crazy schedule, fabric all over the house, and the carryout meals when I'm facing yet another deadline. I couldn't do it without your support.

Sarah

**DOLORES SMITH**
I would like to recognize the ladies who help Sarah and me run our quilt shop. Thank you, Dawn, Sue, Gladys, Lori, Carole, Deanna, April, Jane, Delana, Madison, and Shannen. Each one has helped make the shop what it is today. But I especially want to honor the nurses in this world who have comforted patients. I am also thankful for my husband, Brian, son, Kyle, and soon-to-be daughter-in-law, Dharti, who encourage me and give me the freedom to follow my dreams. To my special guardian angels—son, Ryan; soulmate, Breigha; and my father, Vernon—you will never be forgotten.

With all my love and appreciation,

Dolores

# ACKNOWLEDGMENTS

Writing and publishing a book requires the help and support of many people beyond the authors. We want to specifically thank the following individuals:

Pati Violick of Marcus Fabrics, Clifford Quibell of Andover Fabrics, and Lissa Alexander of Moda Fabrics for generously supplying us with many of the gorgeous fabrics seen in the featured quilts.

Connie Gresham for her amazing machine quilting skills and her patience in working with all of our last-minute deadlines.

Doug Weaver for allowing us to share our vision with fellow quilters via the fantastic books published by Kansas City Star Quilts.

Kimber Mitchell, our editor, who organized our thoughts and provided valuable input about the final product.

Aaron Leimkuehler, our photographer, for showcasing the quilts with his excellent photography.

Bob Deck, our designer, whose creative flair made this book a feast for the eyes.

Lon Eric Craven, illustrator, who translated our drawings into user-friendly illustrations.

Deanna Hodson, our technical editor, whose attention to detail improved the accuracy of our patterns.

Jo Ann Groves, our photo editor, who fine-tuned the photos in this book.

# INTRODUCTION

While much is written about the men and boys who served in some capacity during the Civil War, much less attention has been focused on the role of women during that time. At least 2,000 women worked as nurses, often as volunteers, both in hospitals and near battle sites during the course of the war. Some believe the actual number of women who served was much higher, perhaps as many as 8,000, but because the women were unpaid, their actual work was seldom recorded in military records. These women provided a valuable service to the country, and their work also served to indirectly promote the cause of women's rights.

By piecing together historical records and actual diary entries from nine Civil War nurses, this book illustrates what women of the era experienced. Please note that the grammar and punctuation in the excerpts taken from these historical documents have been left in their original state to reflect the writing of the time. *Comfort and Devotion* is a tribute to the undaunted women who found a way to serve their country, even when such service was not sought or even welcomed. While not trained as a nurse, Clara Barton tended to many wounded soldiers and went on to establish the Red Cross in the United States. In 1892, she wrote a poem about her fellow nurses entitled, "The Women Who Went to the Field." An excerpt appears below and on the following page.

*Dolores        Sarah*

*The women who went to the field, you say,*
*The women who went to the field; and pray*
*What did they go for? just to be in the way!-*
*They'd not know the difference betwixt work and play,*
*What did they know about war anyway?*
*What could they do? - of what use could they be?*
*They would scream at the sight of a gun, don't you see? . . .*
*When the charge is rammed home and the fire belches hot;-*
*They never will wait for the answering shot.*
*They would faint at the first drop of blood, in their sight.*
*What fun for us boys,-(ere we enter the fight;)*
*They might pick some lint, and tear up some sheets,*
*And make us some jellies, and send on their sweets,*
*And knit some soft socks for Uncle Sam's shoes,*
*And write us some letters, and tell us the news.*
*And thus it was settled by common consent,*
*That husbands, or brothers, or whoever went,*

That the place for the women was in their own homes,
There to patiently wait until victory comes.
But later, it chanced, just how no one knew,
That the lines slipped a bit, and some 'gan to crowd through;
And they went, - where did they go? - Ah; where did they not?
Show us the battle, - the field, - or the spot
Where the groans of the wounded rang out on the air
That her ear caught it not, and her hand was not there,
Who wiped the death sweat from the cold, clammy brow,
And sent home the message; - "'Tis well with him now"?
Who watched in the tents, whilst the fever fires burned,
And the pain-tossing limbs in agony turned,
And wet the parched tongue, calmed delirium's strife
Till the dying lips murmured, "My Mother," "My Wife"!
And who were they all? - They were many, my men:
Their record was kept by no tabular pen:
Did these women quail at the sight of a gun?
Will some soldier tell us of one he saw run?
Will he glance at the boats on the great western flood,
At Pittsburgh and Shiloh, did they faint at the blood? . . .
And these were the women who went to the war:
The women of question; what did they go for?
Because in their hearts God had planted the seed
Of pity for woe, and help for its need;
They saw, in high purpose, a duty to do,
And the armor of right broke the barriers through.
Uninvited, unaided, unsanctioned ofttimes,
With pass, or without it, they pressed on the lines;
They pressed, they implored, till they ran the lines through,
And this was the "running" the men saw them do.
'T was a hampered work, its worth largely lost;
'T was hindrance, and pain, and effort, and cost:
But through these came knowledge, - knowledge is power.-
And never again in the deadliest hour
Of war or of peace shall we be so beset
To accomplish the purpose our spirits have met.
And what would they do if war came again?
The scarlet cross floats where all was blank then.
They would bind on their "brassards" and march to the fray,
And the man liveth not who could say to them nay;
They would stand with you now, as they stood with you then,
The nurses, consolers, and saviors of men.

*Unidentified nurse*

# GENERAL INSTRUCTIONS

The quilts in this book are constructed with rotary cutting and machine piecing. The wool pillow on page 76 is hand appliquéd. In the instructions below, we will share our favorite methods and tips. Feel free to adapt any of them to suit yourself. We firmly believe that the best quilt is a finished quilt. We love antique and primitive quilts, so we seldom worry about perfectly lining up stripes or rotating every single piece so the fabric is perfectly oriented. At the same time, we value sharp points and accurately-sized blocks. These tips should aid in achieving those goals.

## FABRIC

The quality of your fabric makes a difference in the finished result! Your local quilt shop will generally sell top quality, 100% cotton fabrics suitable for piecing and quilting. If you're going to take time to make a quilt, why not invest in the best materials possible so your work lasts to pass down to those special loved ones?

## PRE-WASHING

The eternal debate of whether to pre-wash will always have proponents on each side of the argument. Personally, we never pre-wash fabric. Fabric fresh off the bolt generally has a crisp feel and fewer wrinkles than something that has been washed and dried. Before cutting, we iron the fabric with a hot iron, steam, and spray starch. This combination will generally reveal if any fabric is a candidate for excessive shrinking. Once a quilt is finished, dye-catcher sheets, such as the Shout Color Catcher, can be thrown into the washing machine to catch any dye that isn't stable.

## SEAM ALLOWANCE

Make sure you are sewing with an accurate ¼" seam allowance. All the patterns in this book require a ¼" seam allowance. One simple way to make sure you have an accurate seam allowance is to cut 3—1½" x 9" strips, sew them together, and measure the center strip. If it measures 1" exactly, then your seam allowance is good to go! If not, try placing a piece of tape in front of your presser foot ¼" away from where the needle hits the fabric to use as a guide, then try again. Continue experimenting with the placement of the tape until that center strip is 1" wide.

## PRESSING

In general, press seams to the darker fabric. We like to press after each piecing step.

## APPLIQUÉ

The template provided for the wool pillow on page 79 shows the finished edge of the piece as a solid line. Depending on your preferred method of appliqué, you can prepare templates and appliqué as desired. For the pillow, Dolores used a running stitch and a whipstitch to attach the appliqué shapes to the background. Refer to your local library or quilt shop for instruction books on appliqué methods.

# DOROTHEA DIX

In 1861, the field of nursing hardly existed for men or women. Men trained as doctors, but little thought was given to formally training those individuals who would offer continued care for sick or wounded individuals. Since women were not offered many educational opportunities of any kind in the mid 1800s, the field of medicine had few female practitioners. Society believed that women were too frail and weak to adequately work in medicine. Thus, when the Civil War began, few individuals had the professional training needed to serve as nurses.

As it became apparent that the war was not going to be resolved quickly, more men were drafted into military service and thus taken away from their potential roles as healthcare providers. A report to the Committee on Nurses Corp for the Army of the Cumberland highlighted this problem, finding that:

> The supply of nurses-both male and female-is inadequate to the necessities of the service . . . The "Regulations" allow one nurse for every ten patients on beds-but the present "orders" take away all able bodied men, and supply their places with invalids, disqualified by lack of training, and physical disability, . . . the efficiency diminished one half or two thirds.

In essence, the military initially tried to care for its fallen soldiers with other soldiers who were convalescing from their own injuries. As this picture began to emerge, Dorothea Dix organized a march on Washington, D.C., in April 1861 to demand that women be allowed to care for wounded soldiers. Prior to the war, Dix had advocated for better care for the mentally ill, so she was a familiar face to Washington's leaders.

Born April 4, 1802, Dix first worked as a teacher, even opening a free school for poor girls. She was active in many social causes, and while teaching Sunday School at a women's prison, she discovered how poorly the mentally ill inmates were treated. She immediately began a campaign to secure better conditions in the prisons and also won funding for new or expanded hospitals to care for the mentally ill rather than prisons. Dix successfully lobbied Congress for a grant of more than 12 million acres of land to be used as a public endowment for the benefit of the mentally ill, as well as the blind and deaf. However, after Congressional approval in 1854, President Franklin Pierce vetoed the bill. Dix was extremely disappointed by the setback and for a few years went to Europe where she toured hospitals and prisons and worked on behalf of the mentally ill in many countries.

She returned to the United States, and when the Civil War began, she asked Washington lawmakers to allow women to have a role in caring for wounded soldiers. Dix was named Superintendent of Nursing for the U.S. Army in 1861. In that role, she recruited other female nurses, organized field hospitals, and oversaw the care of many Union soldiers. Dix was known for her stern demeanor and strict rules. Initially, she accepted only women who were "plain" looking and more than 30 years of age. She required her nurses to wear only brown or black dresses with no jewelry or decorative features. However, as it became clear that the war was going to last for some time and as casualties grew, she relaxed these standards and soon accepted any woman who applied to serve.

Even though Dix was appointed to her role through a formal nomination by the military, neither she nor her recruits received formal military commissions and thus earned no military pension. Female nurses were paid 40 cents a day plus rations, housing, and transportation. In contrast, male nurses received more than double that rate of pay and other benefits, including a pension.

*Dorothea Dix was recognized as a "Great American" with a commemorative stamp on September 23, 1983.*

Dix's strong personality often put her in conflict with male doctors and hospital administrators. In October 1863, the Secretary of War effectively rescinded much of her authority and gave the U.S. Surgeon General the right to appoint war-time nurses and allowed each hospital to retain jurisdiction over its own nurses. Dix was dismayed by these changes, but it did not affect her commitment to caring for wounded soldiers. Even without a formal post or pay, she worked throughout the remainder of the war and then continued an additional 18 months into 1867, helping wounded soldiers recover and re-enter everyday life.

**"In a world where there is so much to be done, I felt strongly impressed that there must be something for me to do."**
**— Dorothea Dix**

# METRO BASKETS

*Designed and made by Sarah Maxwell*

**Finished quilt size:** 55" x 64"
**Finished block size:** 6" x 6"

# METRO BASKETS

A simple variation of a basket block offers a great opportunity to play with color combinations in this 30-block quilt. For a variety of colors from pinks and blues to greens and grays, I selected Metropolitan Fair fabrics by Barbara Brackman. Choose a fabric line you love and enjoy combining fabrics in the blocks.

## Fabric Requirements

+ 2 yards total of assorted light prints for basket backgrounds
+ 3 yards total of assorted medium and dark prints for baskets
+ ⅞ yard light gray floral for setting triangles and corner triangles
+ ½ yard dark gray print for inner border
+ 1⅜ yards large-scale print for outer border
+ ⅝ yard dark blue print for binding

## Cutting Instructions

*Block cutting instructions below are for one block only. For each basket block, select one light background print and one medium or dark print.*

**From light print, cut:**
• 3—2⅞" squares, then cut each in half diagonally once for a total of six half-square triangles for block

**From medium or dark print, cut:**
• 2—2⅞" squares, then cut each in half diagonally once for a total of four half-square triangles for block (you won't need one of the triangles)
• 1—6⅞" square, then cut it in half diagonally once to create two half-square triangles for block (you won't need one of the triangles, so consider using it in a different block)

**From light gray floral, cut:**
• 5—9¾" squares, then cut each in half diagonally twice for a total of 20 setting triangles (you won't need two of the triangles)
• 2—5⅛" squares, then cut each in half diagonally once for a total of four corner triangles

**From dark gray print, cut:**
• 8—2" strips the width of fabric for inner border

**From large-scale blue print, cut:**
• 8—5½" the width of fabric for outer border

**From dark blue print, cut:**
• 8—2½" strips the width of fabric for binding

## BLOCKS

1. With right sides together, layer a light print half-square triangle with a dark print half-square triangle. Using a ¼" seam allowance, sew along the long side of the triangles to create a half-square triangle unit. Press the seam toward the dark print. Repeat to make a total of three half-square triangle units.

2. Referring to the following diagram, sew together three half-square triangle units from step 1 and three light print triangles. Press the seams in the top row to the right and those in the second row to the left.

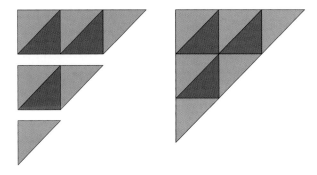

3. Sew a large dark print triangle to the bottom of the unit from step 2.

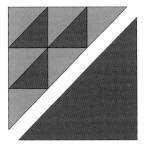

4. Repeat steps 1–3 to make a total of 30 basket blocks, varying the fabric combinations with each block.

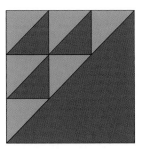

## Quilt Assembly

1. Referring to the quilt assembly diagram on page 17, lay out the basket blocks, setting triangles, and corner triangles.

2. Referring to the quilt assembly diagram, sew the units from step 1 into diagonal rows, paying careful attention to the orientation of the blocks. Press the seams of each row in alternate directions.

3. Join the rows to complete the quilt center, which should measure 43" x 51½".

4. Measure the quilt center from top to bottom through the center. Piece two 2"-wide dark gray print strips end to end, then cut to match that measurement. Repeat to make a second inner border strip. Referring to the quilt assembly diagram, sew these two strips to the sides of the quilt center. Press the seams toward the inner border.

5. Measure the quilt top from side to side through the center (including the borders you just added). Piece two 2"-wide dark gray print strips end to end, then cut to match that measurement. Repeat to make a second inner border strip. Referring to the quilt assembly diagram, sew these two strips to the top and bottom of the quilt top. Press the seams toward the inner border.

6. Measure the quilt top from top to bottom through the center. Piece two 5½"-wide large-scale blue print strips end to end, then cut to match that measurement. Repeat to make a second outer border strip. Referring to the quilt assembly diagram, sew these two strips to the sides of the quilt top. Press the seams toward the outer border.

7. Measure the quilt top from side to side through the center (including the borders you just added). Piece two 5½"-wide large-scale blue print strips end to end, then cut to match that measurement. Repeat to make a second outer border strip. Referring to the quilt assembly diagram, sew these two strips to the top and bottom of the quilt top. Press the seams toward the outer border.

8. Sandwich the quilt top, batting, and backing; baste. Quilt as desired, then bind.

*Assembly Diagram*

# CLARA BARTON

Born Clarissa Harlowe Barton on December 25, 1821, Clara asserted her independence early on when she asked to be called "Clara" instead of her given name. At a time when few women worked outside of the home, she secured a job in the U.S. Patent Office and was working there when the Civil War began. As Clara watched the influx of soldiers into Washington, D.C., she immediately recognized the need for some organization amidst all the chaos. Soon she was visiting soldiers in the area and collecting supplies for their use.

Convinced that if conditions in towns were so poor for the troops, it must be worse on the battlefield, Barton lobbied the government until she obtained permission to travel to battlefields. One night she showed up on a Virginia battlefield at midnight with a wagon full of supplies. The surgeon on duty wrote: "I thought that night if heaven ever sent out a[n]... angel, she must be one— her assistance was so timely." This writing prompted her nickname, "Angel of the Battlefield." As the war progressed, she followed troops and tended the wounded following the battles of Fairfax Station, Chantilly, Harpers Ferry, South Mountain, Antietam, Fredericksburg, Charleston, Petersburg, and Cold Harbor.

Barton was fearless and refused to stay back from actual conflict. During the Battle of Antietam, she actually tended the wounded in the midst of the battle. Commenting on her need to be available during the conflict itself, she wrote: "I always tried . . . to succor the wounded until medical aid and supplies could come up—I could run the risk; it made no difference to anyone if I were shot or taken prisoner."

Barton was frustrated by the incompetence and greed rampant in the upper echelons of the military. As she watched the soldiers go hungry and their lack of clothing and other basic supplies, she noticed that some officers seemed to be profiting from their involvement in the war. Never one to sit idly by, Clara took action. Her diary entry tells the story:

No one has forgotten the heart-sickness which spread over the entire country as the busy wires flashed the dire tidings of the terrible destitution and suffering of the wounded of the Wilderness whom I attended as they lay in Fredericksburg. But you may never have known how many hundredfold of these ills were augmented by the conduct of improper, heartless, unfaithful officers in the immediate command of the city and upon whose actions and indecisions depended entirely the care, food, shelter, comfort, and lives of that whole city of wounded men. One of the highest officers there has since been convicted a traitor. And another, a little dapper captain quartered with the owners of one of the finest mansions in the town, boasted that he had changed his opinion since entering the city the day before; that it was in fact a pretty hard thing for refined people like the people of Fredericksburg to be compelled to open their homes and admit these "dirty, lousy, common soldiers," and that he was not going to compel it.

This I heard him say, and waited until I saw him make his words good, till I saw, crowded into one old sunken hotel, lying helpless upon its bare, wet, bloody floors, five hundred fainting men hold up their cold, bloodless, dingy hands, as I passed, and beg me in Heaven's name for a cracker to keep them from starving (and I had none); or to give them a cup that they might have something to drink water from, if they could get it (and I had no cup and could get none); till I saw two hundred six-mule army wagons in a line, ranged down the street to headquarters, and reaching so far out on the Wilderness road that I never found the end of it; every wagon crowded with wounded men, stopped, standing in the rain and mud, wrenched back and forth by the restless, hungry animals all night from four o'clock in the afternoon till eight the next morning and how much longer I, know not . . . I remembered one man who would set it right, if he knew it, who possessed the power and who would believe me if I told him . . . Henry Wilson, chairman of the Military Committee of the Senate . . .

He listened to the story of suffering and faithlessness, and hurried from my presence, with lips compressed and face like ashes. At ten he stood in the War Department. They could not credit his report. He must have been deceived by some frightened villain. No official report of unusual suffering had reached them. Nothing had been called for by the military authorities commanding Fredericksburg.

Mr. Wilson assured them that the officers in trust there were not to be relied upon. They were faithless, overcome by the blandishments of the wily inhabitants. Still the Department doubted. It was then that he proved that my confidence in his firmness was not misplaced, as, facing his doubters he replies: "One of two things will have to be done-either you will send someone tonight with the power to investigate and correct the abuses of our wounded men at Fredericksburg, or the Senate will send someone tomorrow."

This threat recalled their scattered senses.

At two o'clock in the morning the Quartermaster-General and staff galloped to the 6th Street wharf under orders; at ten they were in Fredericksburg. At noon the wounded men were fed from the food of the city and the houses were opened to the "dirty, lousy soldiers" of the Union Army.

Both railroad and canal were opened. In three days, I returned with carloads of supplies. No more jolting in army wagons! And every man who left Fredericksburg by boat or by car owes it to the firm decision of one man that his grating bones were not dragged ten miles across the country or left to bleach-in the sands of that city.

Throughout the war, Clara worked hard to expose corruption and ease the plight of the soldier. Following the war, she worked for four years helping families reconnect with missing soldiers. With help from President Lincoln, she established the Office of Correspondence with Friends of the Missing Men of the United States Army, which helped locate 22,000 missing men and answered more than 63,000 letters seeking information about their loved ones.

In 1869, Barton traveled to Europe to rest and recover from her years of service. While there she learned about the Red Cross, which sought international agreements among countries guaranteeing basic rights for sick or wounded soldiers during wartime without regard to nationality. Barton was intrigued by the idea and convinced America should enter into an agreement with the International Red Cross. She spent five years lobbying for the concept before finally convincing President Chester Arthur to sign the agreement in 1881. Barton spent the next 20 years working for the American Red Cross, responding to natural disasters and sending supplies abroad to other countries in need.

# RED CROSS

*Designed by Sarah Maxwell and made by Dolores Smith*

Finished quilt size: 76¾" x 89⅜"

Finished block size: 9" x 9"

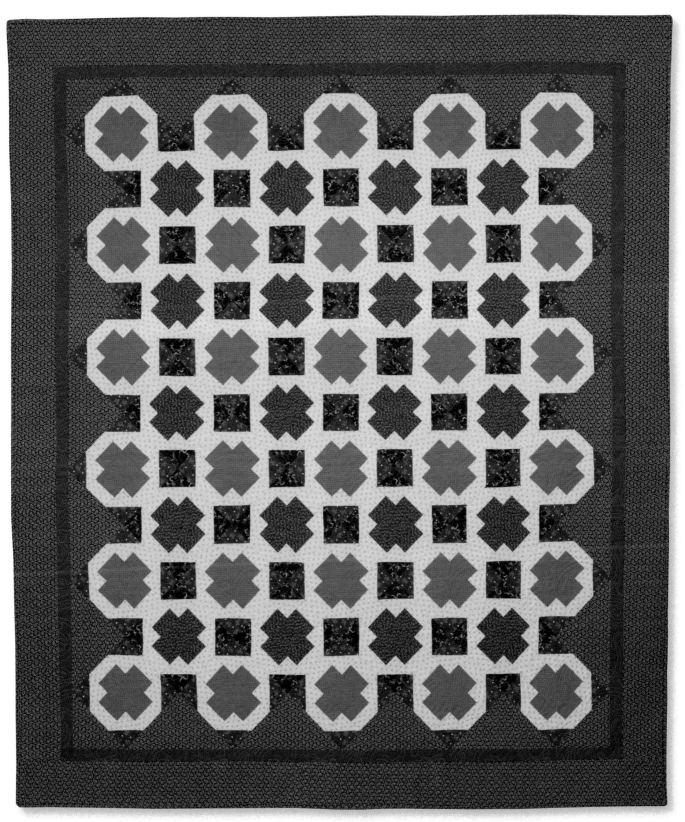

# RED CROSS

The Red Cross motif in this quilt pays tribute to Clara Barton, who founded the International Red Cross. At a time when women were discouraged from seeking an education or working, Clara cared fearlessly for wounded Civil War soldiers.

## Fabric Requirements

+ ¾ yard red print 1 for Block As
+ ⅝ yard black print for Block As
+ 1 yard cheddar print for Block Bs
+ ⅞ yard red print 2 for Block Bs
+ 2⅝ yards shirting for Block As and Bs
+ ⅝ yard red print 3 for inner border
+ 3½ yards black/red print for outer border and binding

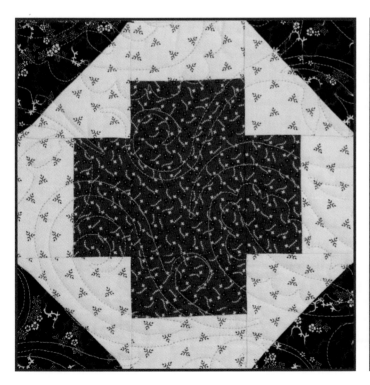

BLOCK A

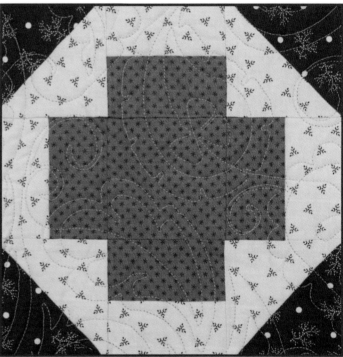

BLOCK B

# Cutting Instructions

*Block cutting instructions below are for one block only.*

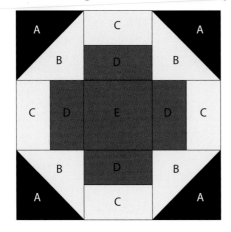 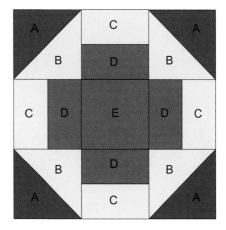

**From black print, cut:**
- 2—3⅞" squares (A), then cut each in half diagonally once for Block A

**From shirting, cut:**
- 2—3⅞" squares (B), then cut each in half diagonally once for Block A
- 4—2" x 3½" rectangles (C) for Block A
- 2—3⅞" squares (B), then cut each in half diagonally once for Block B
- 4—2" x 3½" rectangles (C) for Block B

**From red print 1, cut:**
- 4—2" x 3½" rectangles (D) for Block A
- 1—3½" square (E) for Block A

**From red print 2, cut:**
- 2—3⅞" squares (A), then cut each in half diagonally once for Block B

**From red print 3, cut:**
- 8—2" strips the width of fabric for inner border

**From cheddar print, cut:**
- 4—2" x 3½" rectangles (D) for Block B
- 1—3½" square (E) for Block B

**From black/red print, cut:**
- 5—13⅞" squares, then cut each in half diagonally twice for a total of 20 setting triangles (you won't need two of the triangles)
- 2—7¼" squares, then cut each in half diagonally once for a total of four corner triangles
- 9—5½" strips the width of fabric for outer border
- 9—2½" strips the width of fabric for binding

## *Sewing Instructions*

### BLOCK A

1. With right sides together, layer a black print triangle and shirting triangle. Using a ¼" seam allowance, sew them together along the long side to create a half-square triangle unit. Press the seam toward the black print. Repeat to make a total of four half-square triangle units.

2. With right sides together, layer a red print 1 rectangle and shirting rectangle. Using a ¼" seam allowance, sew the rectangles together along the long side. Press the seam toward the red print 1. Repeat to make a total of four of these units.

3. Referring to the following diagram, sew together the four half-square triangle units, four units from step 2, and a 3½" red print 1 square to complete the block.

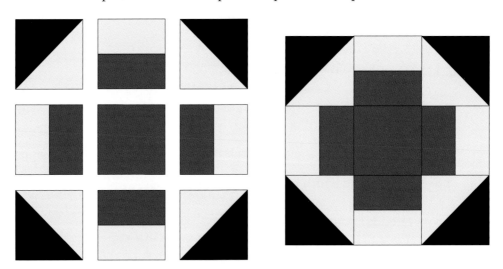

4. Repeat steps 1–3 to make a total of 20 Block As.

## BLOCK B

1. With right sides together, layer a red print 2 triangle and shirting triangle. Using a ¼" seam allowance, sew them together along the long side to create a half-square triangle unit. Press the seam toward the red print 2. Repeat to make a total of four half-square triangle units.

2. With right sides together, layer a cheddar print rectangle and shirting rectangle. Using a ¼" seam allowance, sew the rectangles together along the long side. Press the seam toward the cheddar print. Repeat to make a total of four of these units.

3. Referring to the following diagram, sew together the four half-square triangle units, four units from step 2, and a 3½" cheddar print square to complete the block.

4. Repeat steps 1–3 to make a total of 30 Block Bs.

# Quilt Assembly

1. Referring to the quilt assembly diagram on page 27, lay out the 20 Block As, 30 Block Bs, setting triangles, and corner triangles. Sew them together into rows, being careful to match the corners where the Hourglass designs form. Press the seams in alternate directions.

2. Join the rows to create the quilt center, which should measure 64¼" x 76¾".

3. Measure the quilt center from top to bottom through the center. Piece two 2"-wide red print 3 strips end to end, then cut to match that measurement. Repeat to make a second inner border strip. Referring to the quilt assembly diagram, sew these two strips to the sides of the quilt center. Press the seams toward the inner border.

4. Measure the quilt top from side to side through the center (including the borders you just added). Piece two 2"-wide red print 3 strips end to end, then cut to match that measurement. Repeat to make a second inner border strip. Referring to the quilt assembly diagram, sew these two strips to the top and bottom of the quilt top. Press the seams toward the inner border.

5. Measure the quilt top from top to bottom through the center. Piece three 5½"-wide black/red print strips end to end, then cut to match that measurement. Repeat with the remaining portion of the strip you just cut, plus two 5½"-wide strips to make a second outer border strip. Referring to the quilt assembly diagram, sew these two strips to the sides of the quilt top. Press the seams toward the outer border.

6. Measure the quilt top from side to side through the center (including the borders you just added). Piece two 5½"-wide black/red print strips end to end, then cut to match that measurement. Repeat to make a second outer border strip. Referring to the quilt assembly diagram, sew these two strips to the top and bottom of the quilt top. Press the seams toward the outer border.

7. Sandwich the quilt top, batting, and backing; baste. Quilt as desired, then bind.

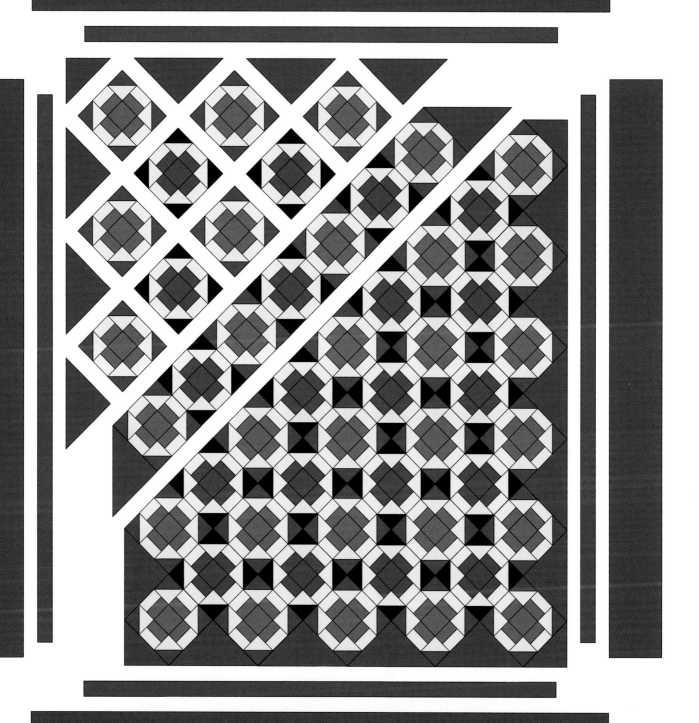

*Assembly Diagram*

# ELIZA GILLESPIE

Born in 1824, Eliza Maria Gillespie was the daughter of a prominent Pennsylvania family. In 1853, she followed a religious calling by joining the Sisters of the Holy Cross. She took the name Sister Angela, and soon her exceptional leadership skills were recognized and she was named director of St. Mary's Academy.

In October 1861, General Grant requested help for wounded soldiers, and the request was relayed to the Academy. Mother Angela immediately organized a group of five sisters who traveled to Illinois to report to General Ulysses S. Grant. The sisters were initially sent to Paducah, Kentucky, where they organized three field hospitals. The women's hard work and organizational skills soon brought order to the hospitals, and they earned the grudging respect of the surgeons.

Mother Angela was recognized for her unfailing devotion to her duties. One nurse recalled an incident that characterized Mother Angela's service:

**Mother Angela was assisting Doctor Franklin with a difficult operation, the precise accuracy of which would determine the life or death of a soldier. A little chloroform had to suffice to dull the agony of the probing. Both surgeon and assistant leaned intently over the patient. Suddenly a red drop fell on Mother Angela's white coif. Another and still another fell until a small stream was seeping through the ceiling. But true to her Celtic ancestry Mother Angela remained motionless, with thoughts concentrated on the delicate surgery. At last the final stitch was taken; two heads rose simultaneously. Not until then did the doctor realize that a crimson rivulet from the floor above had fallen steadily upon our Mother's devoted head, bathing coif, face, and shoulders in blood.**

Disturbed by the lack of supplies and the poor food given to soldiers, she quickly used her family connections to procure better provisions for the hospitals. The wounded men were soon eating a healthy variety of rice, eggs, milk, and chicken instead of rotten pork and stale bread. Mother Angela returned to St. Mary's Academy in December to recruit more nurses. As her duties expanded, Mother Angela soon found herself directing 60 nuns who were responsible for 1,400 men.

Respected by all, Mother Angela received a tribute from General Grant who commented that Mother Angela was "a woman of rare charm of manner, unusual ability, and exceptional executive talents."

One of her fellow nurses wrote:

**There are some people who can inspire others to do what ordinarily speaking is impossible; Mother Angela was one of these. Her faith and courage never recognized limitations; hence the nature, the magnitude of her achievements and those of her Sisters.**

# RIDING *the* RAILS

*Designed and made by Sarah Maxwell*

Finished quilt size: 73½" x 95"
Finished block size: 7½" x 7½"

# RIDING *the* RAILS

The Rail Fence pattern is a classic that works well for showcasing a trio of color combinations. My version features 83 blocks in an on-point setting. By rotating the blocks, zigzags of color appear.

## Fabric Requirements

+ 1⅞ yards each of three different prints for blocks (the three fabrics should be different colors and values to create a zigzag effect)
+ 1 yard medium to light print for setting triangles and corner triangles
+ 1¾ yards large-scale print for outer border
+ ¾ yard dark print or plaid for binding

## Cutting Instructions

From *each* of three prints, cut:
• 16—3" strips the width of fabric for blocks

From medium to light prints, cut:
• 6—11⅞" squares, then cut each in half diagonally twice for a total of 24 setting triangles
• 2—6⅛" squares, then cut each in half diagonally once for a total of four corner triangles

From large scale-print, cut:
• 10—5½" strips the width of fabric for border

From dark print or plaid, cut:
• 10—2½" strips the width of fabric for binding

# *Sewing Instructions*

## BLOCKS

Sew together three different colored 3"-wide strips from the cutting list, being sure to keep the fabrics arranged in the same order in each strip set. From each strip set, cut 5—8" squares for a total of 83 squares.

# *Quilt Assembly*

1. Referring to the quilt assembly diagram on page 32, lay out the 83 blocks, paying careful attention to their orientation to create the necessary zigzag effect.

2. Referring to the quilt assembly diagram, sew together the blocks into diagonal rows. Press the seams of each of the rows in alternate directions.

3. Join the rows to create the quilt center, which should measure 64" x 85½".

4. Measure the quilt center from top to bottom through the center. Piece three 5½"-wide large-scale print strips end to end, then cut to match that measurement. Repeat to make a second outer border strip. Referring to the quilt assembly diagram, sew these two strips to the sides of the quilt center. Press the seams toward the border.

5. Measure the quilt top from side to side through the center (including the borders you just added). Piece two 5½"-wide large-scale print strips end to end, then cut to match that measurement. Repeat to make a second outer border strip. Referring to the quilt assembly diagram, sew these two strips to the top and bottom of the quilt top. Press the seams toward the border.

6. Sandwich the quilt top, batting, and backing; baste. Quilt as desired, then bind.

*Assembly Diagram*

# MARY ANN BICKERDYKE

Mary Ann Bickerdyke, born July 19, 1817, was an ordinary woman of the 1800s until her mid 40s. She worked as a household servant until her marriage at age 30. The couple settled in Galesburg, Illinois, and became members of the church where Reverend Edward Beecher served. He was the brother of Harriet Beecher Stowe, author of *Uncle Tom's Cabin.* She had two children, one of whom, a daughter, died in infancy. Following that event, Bickerdyke became fascinated with medical literature and began reading everything about medicine that she could find.

Shortly after the Civil War started, Reverend Beecher shared a letter about the poor medical care available to Union soldiers on the battlefield, and Mary Ann decided to focus all of her efforts on improving the situation. Recently widowed, she left two young sons in the care of a friend and, after gathering supplies from her neighbors, she made her way to the nearest Army base in Cairo, Illinois, and saw first-hand just how bad the conditions were. She wrote:

**It was far worse than the doctor's faltering pen had been able to picture. Ten men were crowded into the first tent, one or two on cots, most of them on straw pallets spread with an army blanket or a winter overcoat. The beds were so close together that there was scarcely room to move between them. The mud floor was foul with human excrement. A swarm of blue-bottle flies circled low over the sufferers, keeping up an angry humming almost as loud as the groans and moans and painful labored breathing. The patients lay in shirts and underdrawers, filthy with vomit, rank with perspiration. On a cot near the door a human scarecrow sat, dressed like the others, feebly stirring the fetid air with a palm-leaf fan. At his feet was a tin water pail with dipper. It was empty. It should have been full, for this man was the nurse, and one of his duties was to fetch drinking water from the nearest storage barrel. He tottered off the cot as the doctor entered and stood shakily at salute . . . The others [tents] were no different and no better.**

Bickerdyke chose to stay on at the base and took up nursing duties, even though her presence violated the Army ban on women. Over time, she encouraged other local ladies to volunteer their services, and gradually conditions at the base improved. As the war continued, she began to join soldiers on the battlefield and tended to the wounded as they fell in battle, working in make-shift field hospitals. While initially unwelcome, her presence soon became valued by Army doctors. Surgeon J.J. Woodward praised Bickerdyke as "strong as a man, muscles of iron, nerves of finest steel; sensitive, but self-reliant, kind and tender; seeking all for others, nothing for herself."

Finally, after caring for Ulysses S. Grant's own brigade at the Battle of Shiloh, she was hired in an official capacity by the U.S. Sanitary Commission, a federal agency that provided medical services during the war. Traveling from battle to battle, Bickerdyke earned a reputation as a fearless and relentless worker. Following one battle, General "Black Jack" saw a figure carrying a lamp, walking back and forth over the recently vacated battlefield.

He ordered the person brought in for questioning only to find it was Bickerdyke, who explained that she could not rest until she was satisfied that no living man remained on the field. Eventually, Bickerdyke traveled throughout the South with Union forces, even traveling as far south as Atlanta during General William Sherman's march.

When not caring for wounded men, Bickerdyke worked on behalf of the Sanitary Commission to gather donations that could be used in the field hospitals. While explaining to a group of women in New York about how scarce supplies were, she suddenly asked all of the women to remove one of their petticoats so they could be used for bandages.

When the war finally ended, Bickerdyke resigned from the Sanitary Commission, but continued her charitable work on behalf of former soldiers until her death in 1901.

**When answering a surgeon who questioned who gave Bickerdyke the right to work in his hospital, she replied: "I have received my authority from the Lord God Almighty. Have you anything that ranks higher than that?"**

# NEW NATION

*Designed and made by Sarah Maxwell*

Finished quilt size: 64" x 72¼"
Finished block size: 6" x 6"

# NEW NATION

A variety of prints enlivens this Shoofly quilt, which incorporates 40 different fabrics in its 42 blocks.

## Fabric Requirements

+ 2¼–2¾ yards total of assorted light prints for block backgrounds
+ 2¼–2¾ yards total of assorted medium and dark prints for blocks
+ 1 yard light print for alternating setting squares and setting triangles
+ 3¼ yards dark floral for alternating setting squares, setting triangles, outer border, and binding
+ ⅝ yard blue/cream stripe for inner border

## Cutting Instructions

*Block cutting instructions below are for one block only. For each Shoofly block, select one light background print and one medium or dark print.*

**From light print, cut:**
• 2—2⅞" squares, then cut each in half diagonally once for a total of four half-square triangles for blocks
• 4—2½" squares for blocks

**From medium or dark print, cut:**
• 2—2⅞" squares, then cut each in half diagonally once for a total of four half-square triangles for blocks
• 1—2½" square, then cut it in half diagonally once for a total of two half-square triangles for blocks

**From different light print than above, cut:**
• 15—6½" squares for alternating setting squares
• 3—9¾" squares, then cut each in half diagonally twice for a total of 12 setting triangles (you won't need one of the triangles)
• 2—5⅛" squares, then cut them in half diagonally once for a total of four corner triangles (you won't need one of the triangles)

**From dark floral, cut:**
• 15—6½" squares for alternating setting squares
• 3—9¾" squares, then cut each in half diagonally twice for a total of 12 setting triangles (you won't need one of the triangles)
• 1—5⅛" square, then cut it in half diagonally once for a total of two corner triangles (you won't need one of the triangles)
• 8—5½" strips the width of fabric for outer border
• 8—2½" strips the width of fabric for binding

**From blue cream stripe, cut:**
• 8—2" strips the width of fabric for inner border

# Sewing Instructions

## BLOCKS

1. With right sides together, layer a light print half-square triangle with a dark print half-square triangle. Using a ¼" seam allowance, sew along the long side of the triangles to make a half-square triangle unit. Press the seam toward the dark print. Repeat to make a total of four half-square triangle units.

2. Referring to the following diagram, sew together four half-square triangle units from step 1, 4—2½" light print squares, and a 2½" medium or dark print square to create a Shoofly block. Press the seams in the top row to the right, in the middle row to the left, and in the bottom row to the right.

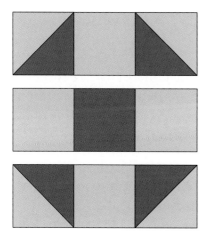

3. Repeat steps 1–2 to create a total of 42 Shoofly blocks, varying the fabric combinations with each block.

## Quilt Assembly

1. Referring to the quilt assembly diagram on page 39, lay out the Shoofly blocks, alternating setting squares, setting triangles, and corner triangles.

2. Referring to the quilt assembly diagram, sew the units from step 1 into diagonal rows.

3. Join the rows to complete the quilt center, which should measure 51½" x 59¾".

4. Measure the quilt center from top to bottom through the center. Piece two 2"-wide blue/cream stripe strips end to end, then cut to match that measurement. Repeat to make a second inner border strip. Referring to the quilt assembly diagram, sew these two strips to the sides of the quilt center. Press the seams toward the inner border.

5. Measure the quilt top from side to side through the center (including the borders you just added). Piece two 2"-wide blue/cream stripe strips end to end, then cut to match that measurement. Repeat to make a second inner border strip. Referring to the quilt assembly diagram, sew these two strips to the top and bottom of the quilt top. Press the seams toward the inner border.

6. Measure the quilt top from top to bottom through the center. Piece two 5½"-wide dark floral strips end to end, then cut to match that measurement. Repeat to make a second outer border strip. Referring to the quilt assembly diagram, sew these two strips to the sides of the quilt top. Press the seams toward the outer border.

7. Measure the quilt top from side to side through the center (including the borders you just added). Piece two 5½"-wide dark floral strips end to end, then cut to match that measurement. Repeat to make a second outer border strip. Referring to the quilt assembly diagram, sew these two strips to the top and bottom of the quilt top. Press the seams toward the outer border.

8. Sandwich the quilt top, batting, and backing; baste. Quilt as desired, then bind.

*Assembly Diagram*

# HANNAH ROPES

Hannah Ropes' work as a nurse during the Civil War is well-documented, as she is one of the few women who maintained extensive journals detailing her experiences. She worked as an abolitionist before the war started. Abandoned by her husband, Hannah moved her children to Lawrence, Kansas, in 1855, thinking she could be more effective in the anti-slavery cause. The Kansas-Nebraska Act of 1854 had established that residents of U.S. territories would be allowed to determine if their area was for or against slavery. She quickly discovered that this Act had made the area very volatile as pro-slavery raiders from Missouri regularly attacked anti-slavery Kansans. The family was forced to keep loaded guns and knives on hand at all times. After several months, Hannah tired of the constant conflict and returned to Massachusetts.

Hannah had sent detailed letters to family members describing life in Kansas, and she used those letters as the basis for a book, *Six Months in Kansas: By a Lady*, which was published in 1856.

When the Civil War began, Hannah offered to work in a hospital on behalf of the Union, and in 1862, she was appointed matron of the Union Hotel Hospital in Washington, D.C., which received many casualties. Louisa May Alcott, best-known as the author of *Little Women*, came to work at the hospital and was soon captivated by Ropes' calm demeanor in the midst of chaos. She wrote:

> In they came, some on stretchers, some in men's arms, some feebly staggering along propped on rude crutches, and one lay stark and still with covered face, as a comrade gave his name to be recorded before they carried him away to the dead house.

> All was hurry and confusion; the hall was full of these wrecks of humanity, for the most exhausted could not reach a bed till duly ticketed and registered; the walls were lined with rows of such as could sit, the floor covered with the more disabled, the steps and doorways filled with helpers and lookers on; the sound of many feet and voices made that usually quiet hour as noisy as noon; and, in the midst of it all, the matron's motherly face brought more comfort to many a poor soul, than the cordial draughts she administered, or the cheery words that welcomed all, making of the hospital a home.

Ropes maintained an extensive diary of her own where she chronicled the daily life of the wounded soldiers and their caretakers. In October 1862, she noted:

> "The poor privates are my special children..." She mourned "the loss they have experienced in health, in spirits, in weakened faith in man, as well as shattered hope in themselves."

Ropes took her duties as matron of the hospital so seriously that she sacrificed much of her own comfort for the soldiers. She declined to join her family for Thanksgiving, and instead focused on rounding up donations so the men could enjoy a nice meal on that holiday. She personally sat with many men as they teetered between life and death, often encouraging them to find a reason to live despite their injuries. In one letter to her daughter, Alice, she explained her work:

> ...The poor fellows are weary of life; a week ago one sent for me to come to him, the nurse telling me he could not live till night. I talked with him awhile, and found he had made up his mind to die. I told him he had no right to any mind about it, no man could know the bounds of his life, and he must consider his, worn and emaciated as it was, the gift of God, for him to use as long as the gift was placed at his command...

Hannah worked tirelessly until she herself caught typhoid fever. Despite daily care from the doctors at the hospital and attention from her fellow nurses, she soon died at the age of 54.

*Civil War hospital tents*

# SQUARED UP

*Designed and made by Sarah Maxwell*

Finished quilt size: 84" x 95"
Finished block size: 8" x 8"

Plaids and homespuns were common fabrics in the 1800s. As supplies became scarce during the Civil War, quilts made of a variety of plaids would have been typical. Simple squares best spotlight the plaid patterns in this quilt of 42 blocks with alternating brown squares in an on-point setting.

## Fabric Requirements

+ 3½ yards assorted light to dark plaids for blocks (¼ yard cuts work well for these)
+ 2¾ yards dark brown print for alternating setting squares, setting triangles, and corner triangles
+ 1 yard light print or plaid for inner border
+ 2⅛ yards large-scale plaid for outer border
+ ¾ yard dark print or plaid for binding

## Cutting Instructions

### From assorted plaids, cut:
• 42—8½" squares for blocks

### From dark brown print, cut:
• 30—8½" squares for alternating setting squares
• 6—12½" squares, then cut each in half diagonally twice for a total of 24 setting triangles (you won't need two of the triangles)
• 2—6½" squares, then cut each in half diagonally once for a total of four corner triangles

### From light print or plaid, cut:
• 8—2½" strips the width of fabric for inner border

### From large-scale plaid, cut:
• 10—6½" strips the width of fabric for outer border

### From dark print, cut:
• 10—2½" strips the width of fabric for binding

## Sewing Instructions

1. Referring to the quilt assembly diagram on page 46, lay out the plaid squares, alternating dark brown print setting squares, setting triangles, and corner triangles.

2. Referring to the quilt assembly diagram, sew the units from step 1 into diagonal rows.

3. Join the rows to complete the quilt center, which should measure 68½" x 79½".

4. Measure the quilt center from top to bottom through the center. Piece two 2½"-wide light print or plaid strips end to end, then cut to match that measurement. Repeat to make a second inner border strip. Referring to the quilt assembly diagram, sew these two strips to the sides of the quilt center. Press the seams toward the inner border.

5. Measure the quilt top from side to side through the center (including the borders you just added). Piece two 2½"-wide light print or plaid strips end to end, then cut to match that measurement. Repeat to make a second inner border strip. Referring to the quilt assembly diagram, sew these two strips to the top and bottom of the quilt top. Press the seams toward the inner border.

6. Measure the quilt top from top to bottom through the center. Piece three 6½"-wide large-scale plaid strips end to end, then cut to match that measurement. Repeat to make a second outer border strip. Referring to the quilt assembly diagram, sew these two strips to the sides of the quilt top. Press the seams toward the outer border.

7. Measure the quilt top from side to side through the center (including the borders you just added). Piece two 6½"-wide large-scale plaid strips end to end, then cut to match that measurement. Repeat to make a second outer border strip. Referring to the quilt assembly diagram, sew these two strips to the top and bottom of the quilt top. Press the seams toward the outer border.

8. Sandwich the quilt top, batting, and backing; baste. Quilt as desired, then bind.

*Assembly Diagram*

# JANE NEWTON WOOLSEY

Jane Newton Woolsey was notable both for her own work during the war and for encouraging her six daughters to also serve in some capacity. Her New York family quickly immersed itself in the war effort, with three of the daughters working as nurses while the rest worked to secure supplies for the troops.

Sisters Jane and Georgy worked both in hospitals throughout New England and on military transport ships. The sisters earned $12 a month for their work and donated much of that back to the hospitals to purchase needed supplies. Sister Eliza also worked in a hospital for a time, but chose to return home when her husband, Colonel Joseph Howland, was wounded.

The Woolsey family was well-connected, which contributed to the success of their fundraising efforts. When Georgy observed that many of the hospitals lacked chaplains, she personally delivered a letter to President Abraham Lincoln, requesting that he take action. Soon after, he responded by appointing seven new chaplains to serve in area hospitals.

Jane Woolsey chronicled her days as a war-time nurse in a book, *Hospital Days*, which was published in 1868. She described how an officer had shared his impression of the nurses at his hospital:

> **She may be totally impervious to ideas of order; she may love "hugger-mugger" and hand-to-mouth ways of getting at direct objects; she may hopelessly muddle the ward returns, and interchange sentiment with the most obnoxious of the stewards, but she will cheerfully sacrifice time, ease, and health to the wants or whims of a wounded man.**

Most poignant in *Hospital Days* is Woolsey's reminiscence about writing letters for soldiers in her care. The families who received these letters were grateful to have news about their kin. One father wrote to Woolsey:

> **I am very glad to know by your writing that my son died among Christians instead of among rebels. My only fears are that he had not the care when he was first taken sick he ought to have had. There are many stories that the sick are not well cared for in many places. I am sure that had any one known how good my son was, they could not have misused him. I should like to know what he said about his home, and also how he was buried. My son is dead; through this rebellion. If I, his father, were Abraham Lincoln, I would kill the cursed cause of it, slavery, before many suns went down. Write all particulars of my son's death and relieve broken hearts.**

When the war ended, Georgy founded the Connecticut Training School for Nurses, sharing her on-the-job experience with other women. She also wrote a book about nursing, which was one of only two nursing handbooks available at the time.

# HOT CROSS BUNS

*Designed and made by Sarah Maxwell*

Finished quilt size: 76" x 88"
Finished block size: 12" x 12"

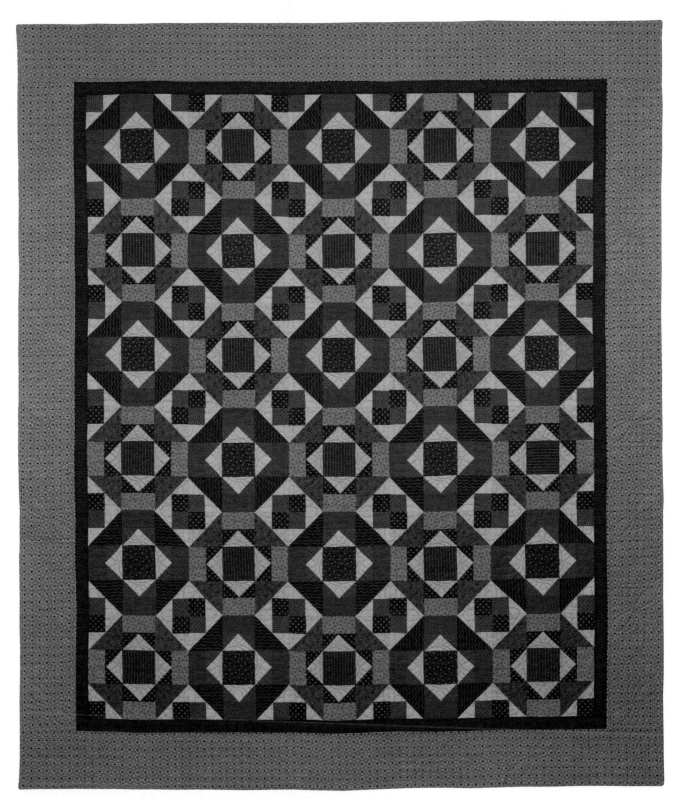

Alternating the colorations of 30 pieced blocks creates an intriguing chain design in this quilt featuring Jo Morton prints by Andover Fabrics.

## *Fabric Requirements*

+ ⅞ yard *each* of two different background prints for Block As and Bs
+ ¾ yard medium orange print for Block As
+ ⅝ yard dark red print for Block As
+ ¾ yard brown print for Block As
+ ⅜ yard red stripe for Block Bs
+ ⅜ yard brown floral for Block As
+ ¾ yard dark brown print for Block Bs
+ ⅝ yard gold ovals print for Block Bs
+ ¾ yard medium brown print for Block Bs
+ ⅝ yard dark brown print for inner border
+ 2¾ yards large-scale cheddar print for outer border and binding

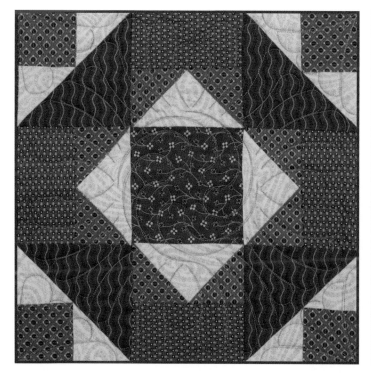

**BLOCK A**

**BLOCK B**

# Cutting Instructions

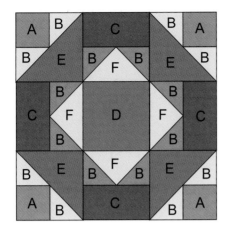

BLOCK A

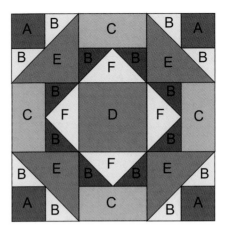

BLOCK B

**From background print 1, cut:**
- 60—2⅞" squares, then cut each in half diagonally once for a total of 120 half-square triangles (B) in Block As
- 15—5¼" squares, then cut each in half diagonally twice for a total of 60 quarter-square triangles (F) in Block As

**From background print 2, cut:**
- 60—2⅞" squares, then cut each in half diagonally once for a total of 120 half-square triangles (B) in Block Bs
- 15—5¼" squares, then cut each in half diagonally twice for a total of 60 quarter-square triangles (F) in Block Bs

**From medium orange print, cut:**
- 60—2⅞" squares, then cut each in half diagonally once for a total of 120 half-square triangles (B) in Block As
- 60—2½" squares (A) in Block As

**From dark red print, cut:**
- 60—2½" x 4½" rectangles (C) in Block As

**From brown floral, cut:**
- 15—4½" squares (D) in Block As

**From brown print, cut:**
- 30—4⅞" squares, then cut each in half diagonally once for a total of 60 half-square triangles (E) in Block As

**From dark brown print, cut:**
- 60—2⅞" squares, then cut each in half diagonally once for a total of 120 half-square triangles (B) for Block Bs
- 60—2½" squares (A) for Block Bs

**From gold ovals print, cut:**
- 60—2½" x 4½" rectangles (C) for Block Bs

**From red stripe, cut:**
- 15—4½" squares (D) for Block Bs

**From medium brown print, cut:**
- 30—4⅞" squares, then cut each in half diagonally once for a total of 60 half-square triangles (E) in Block Bs

**From dark brown print, cut:**
- 8—2" strips the width of fabric for inner border

**From large-scale cheddar print, cut:**
- 8—7" strips the width of fabric for outer border
- 8—2½" strips the width of fabric for binding

# Sewing Instructions

## BLOCK A

1. Sew a (B) background print triangle to two sides of an (A) square. Repeat to make a total of 60 units.

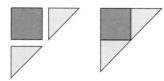

2. Sew an (E) brown print triangle to each of the units from step 1.

3. Sew a (B) medium orange print triangle to each short side of an (F) background print triangle. Repeat to make a total of 60 units.

4. Sew a (C) dark red print rectangle to the top of each unit from step 3.

5. Referring to the following diagram, sew together four units from step 2, four units from step 4, and a 4½" brown floral square to complete the block. Press the seams in the top row to the right, in the middle row to the left, and in the bottom row to the right.

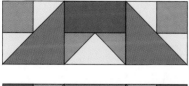

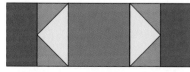

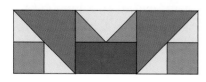

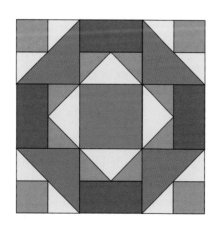

6. Repeat step 5 to make a total of 15 Block As.

## BLOCK B

Referring to the following diagram and the instructions under Block A on page 51, make 15 Block Bs by switching the placement of the prints.

## Quilt Assembly

1. Referring to the quilt assembly diagram on page 53, lay out the Block As and Block Bs, alternating their placements.

2. Referring to the quilt assembly diagram, sew the blocks together into six rows of five blocks each. Press the seams of each row in alternate directions.

3. Join the rows to complete the quilt center, which should measure 60½" x 72½".

4. Measure the quilt center from top to bottom through the center. Piece two 2"-wide dark brown print strips end to end, then cut to match that measurement. Repeat to make a second inner border strip. Referring to the quilt assembly diagram, sew these two strips to the sides of the quilt center. Press the seams toward the inner border.

5. Measure the quilt top from side to side through the center (including the borders you just added). Piece two 2"-wide dark brown print strips end to end, then cut to match that measurement. Repeat to make a second inner border strip. Referring to the quilt assembly diagram, sew these two strips to the top and bottom of the quilt top. Press the seams toward the inner border.

6. Measure the quilt top from top to bottom through the center. Piece two 7"-wide large-scale cheddar print strips end to end, then cut to match that measurement. Repeat to make a second outer border strip. Referring to the quilt assembly diagram, sew these two strips to the sides of the quilt top. Press the seams toward the outer border.

7. Measure the quilt top from side to side through the center (including the borders you just added). Piece two 7"-wide large-scale cheddar print strips end to end, then cut to match that measurement. Repeat to make a second outer border strip. Referring to the quilt assembly diagram, sew these two strips to the top and bottom of the quilt top. Press the seams toward the outer border.

8. Sandwich the quilt top, batting, and backing; baste. Quilt as desired, then bind.

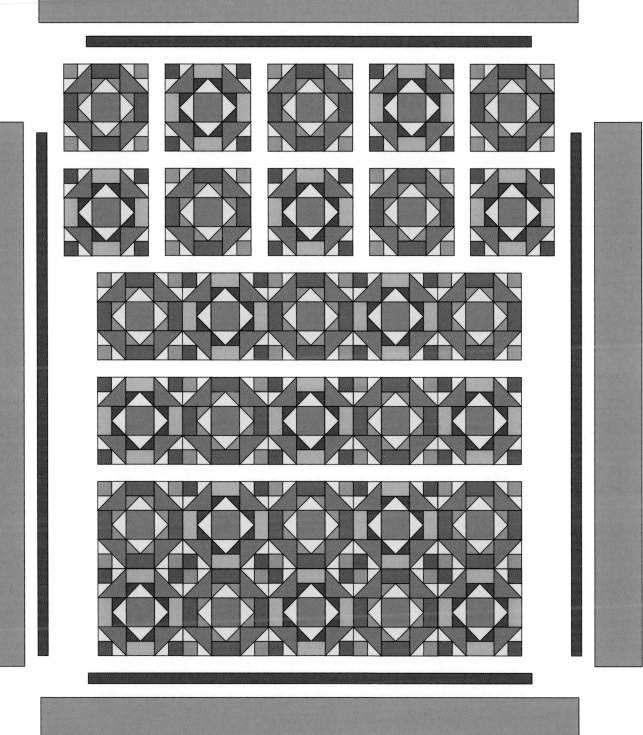

*Assembly Diagram*

# KATE CUMMING

Women of the South also worked as nurses on behalf of the Confederacy. One of the best known is Kate Cumming, a Scotland native who settled in Mobile, Alabama, with her family. When the war began in 1861, her mother and sisters returned to Scotland, but Kate chose to remain in Alabama with her father while her brother joined the Confederate army.

She quickly became active in the local war relief effort, gathering supplies for the soldiers. After hearing a preacher tell of the need for nurses to tend the wounded soldiers, Kate joined a group of 40 women who gathered in Corinth, Mississippi, following the Battle of Shiloh in April 1862. This battle was devastating for both sides with more than 23,000 soldiers wounded or killed. For four months, she tended casualties from this battle and then returned home briefly to assess her future.

Convinced that there was a need for her services, Cumming and two other women traveled throughout the South searching for an Army doctor who would work with women. Finally, she found a doctor in Chattanooga, Tennessee, who welcomed the help. Soon, the Confederacy realized that units with female volunteers had higher survival rates than those without, and they organized a formal nursing program for women. Kate was appointed as a matron for the Army of Tennessee and traveled throughout the South with the troops. Kate kept a detailed journal and described her experiences almost daily. In January 1863, she wrote:

> Another year has commenced, alas! With bloodshed. When will it cease? I ask that question with nothing but echo for my answer . . . The wounded kept coming in last night, till 12 o'clock. Every corner of the hospital is filled with patients . . . All that I or Mrs. Williamson have been able to do for them is to see that they get enough to eat.

Ten months later, it seemed little had changed, as she wrote about the Battle of Chickamauga:

> I found Mr. Hunt's home a very pretty cottage in the midst of a garden, which before the battle had been filled with fine shrubbery and flowers, but was now covered with tents, flies and sheds filled with wounded . . . Every corner of the house was filled with wounded, many of them lying upon bunks made out of the branches of trees, a hard bed at any time, but much more so for these poor wounded veterans . . .

> As we rode out of the yard, I tried to look neither to the right nor the left, for I knew that many eyes were sadly gazing at us from their comfortless sheds and tents. I could do nothing for the poor fellows, and when that is the case, I try to steel my heart against their sorrows. We could see the men cooking out in the pouring rain; a perfect war between the two elements, fire and water. All had a most cheerless aspect. As we rode on, the tents of the various field hospitals came in view, and the thoughts of the inmates and their sufferings added to the gloom. I gazed in the direction of the battlefield and thought of the nameless dead who were there. A nation weeps for them; and on that day nature, like Rachel, was shedding tears for her children because they were not. The awful conflict which had so recently raged between brother and brother was vividly pictured to my mind. Oh! what a field of fratricide was there. It wrings from one the cry of the brave Falkland of old: "Peace! peace! when will it come?"

# FIELDS *of* GREENS

*Designed and made by Sarah Maxwell*

Finished quilt size: 69" x 86"
Finished block size: 12" x 12"

When Marcus Fabrics unveiled Sturbridge Greens, I knew I wanted to incorporate several of the prints into a single quilt. Finding a pattern that showcased them while allowing their relative values to create an interesting pattern became the challenge. The result of my efforts is this quilt, which illustrates how a single color can create a dynamic design. The blocks are set on point and colored differently to create the illusion of floating Nine-Patches.

## Fabric Requirements

The lettered labels below correspond with the fabric swatches at the bottom of the page.

+ ½ yard light floral background print 1 (A) for blocks
+ ½ yard light floral background print 2 (B) for blocks
+ ½ yard light tan print (C) for blocks
+ 2 yards dark green print 1 (D) for blocks, 2nd inner border, and binding
+ ½ yard light tan plumes print (E) for blocks
+ ½ yard medium green ovals print (F) for blocks
+ 1⅛ yards medium green floral (G) for blocks
+ ⅜ yard green/tan print (H) for blocks
+ ½ yard dark green leaf print (I) for blocks
+ 1 yard green squiggle print (J) for blocks
+ ⅜ yard dark green print 3 (K) for blocks
+ ½ yard green/gold floral (L) for blocks, Setting Triangle As, and outer border Nine-Patches
+ ½ yard dark green floral (M) for blocks and Setting Triangle Bs
+ 1¾ yards light green background print (N) for Setting Triangle As and Bs and 1st inner border
+ ⅜ yard light green vine print (O) for outer border Nine-Patches
+ 2 yards dark green print 2 (P) for outer border

A    B    C    D    E    F    G    H

I    J    K    L    M    N    O    P

# Cutting Instructions

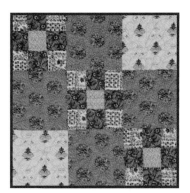

**BLOCK A**

### BLOCK A
*Cutting instructions below are for one block only.*

**From light floral background print 1 (A), cut:**
• 2—4½" squares

**From medium green floral (G), cut:**
• 4—4½" squares

**From light floral background print 2 (B), cut:**
• 12—1⅞" squares

**From light tan (C), cut:**
• 3—1⅞" squares

**From dark green print 3 (K), cut:**
• 12—1⅞" squares

**BLOCK B**

### BLOCK B
*Cutting instructions below are for one block only.*

**From dark green floral (M), cut:**
• 2—4½" squares

**From green squiggle print (J), cut:**
• 4—4½" squares

**From dark green leaf print (I), cut:**
• 12—1⅞" squares

**From green/gold floral (L), cut:**
• 3—1⅞" squares

**From light tan plumes print (E), cut:**
• 12—1⅞" squares

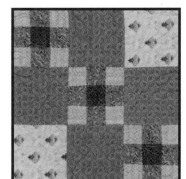

**BLOCK C**

### BLOCK C
*Cutting instructions below are for one block only.*

**From light floral background print 1 (A), cut:**
• 2—4½" squares

**From medium green ovals print (F), cut:**
• 4—4½" squares

**From dark green print 1 (D), cut:**
• 3—1⅞" squares

**From light tan (C), cut:**
• 12—1⅞" squares

**From green/tan print (H), cut:**
• 12—1⅞" squares

## SETTING TRIANGLES

**From dark green leaf print (I), cut:**
• 16—1⅞" squares for Setting Triangle As

**From green/gold floral (L), cut:**
• 4—1⅞" squares for Setting Triangle As

**From light tan plumes print (E), cut:**
• 16—1⅞" squares for Setting Triangle As

**From dark green floral (M), cut:**
• 6—4½" squares for Setting Triangle Bs

**From light green background (N), cut:**
• 10—4⅞" squares, then cut each in half diagonally once for a total of 20 Setting Triangle As and Bs
• 10—3⅜" x 18⅛" strips for Setting Triangle As and Bs. Use the 45-degree marking on your ruler to cut both ends of the strip to form a parallelogram.

## CORNER TRIANGLES

**From light green background (N), cut:**
• 2—9⅜" squares, then cut each in half diagonally once for a total of four corner triangles

## FIRST INNER BORDER

**From light green background (N), cut:**
• 8—1½" strips the width of fabric for first inner border

## SECOND INNER BORDER

**From dark green print 1 (D), cut:**
• 8—2¾" strips the width of fabric for second inner border

## OUTER BORDER

**From green/gold floral (L), cut:**
• 5—1⅞" squares for one Nine-Patch only. You will need to make a total of 14.

**From dark green print 2 (P), cut:**
• 5—7" squares, then cut each in half diagonally twice for a total of 20 setting triangles in outer border
• 8—3¾" squares, then cut each in half diagonally once for a total of 16 corner triangles in outer border
• 8—6½" strips the width of fabric for outer border

**From light green vine (O), cut:**
• 4—1⅞" squares for one Nine-Patch only. You will need to make a total of 14.

## BINDING

**From dark green print 1 (D), cut:**
• 9—2½" strips the width of fabric for binding

## BLOCK A

1. Referring to the following diagram, sew together 4—1⅞" dark green print 3 (K) squares, 4—1⅞" light floral background 2 (B) squares, and 1—1⅞" light tan print (C) square to create a Nine-Patch unit. Repeat to make a total of three Nine-Patch units.

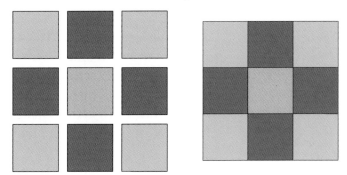

2. Referring to the following diagram, sew together the three Nine-Patch units from step 1, 2—4½" light floral background 1 print (A) squares, and 4—4½" medium green floral (G) squares. Repeat to make a total of eight Block As.

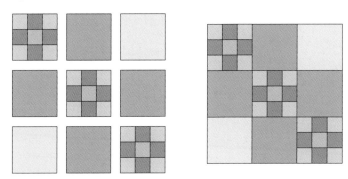

## BLOCK B

Referring to the sewing instructions for Block A, make six Block Bs with the 2—4½" dark green floral (M) squares, 4—4½" green squiggle print (J) squares, 12—1⅞" dark green leaf print (I) squares, 3—1⅞" green/gold floral (L) squares, and 12—1⅞" light tan plumes print (E) squares (the 1⅞" squares are used to make the Nine-Patch units).

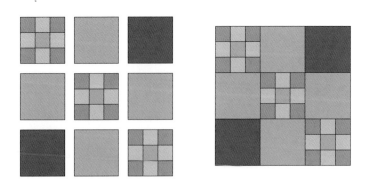

# BLOCK C

Referring to the sewing instructions for Block A, make four Block Cs with the 2—4½" light floral background 1 print (A) squares, 4—4½" medium green ovals print (F) squares, 3—1⅞" dark green print 1 (D) squares, and 12—1⅞" green/tan print (H) squares (the 1⅞" squares are used to create the Nine-Patch units).

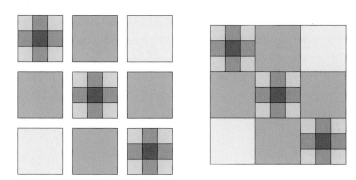

# SETTING TRIANGLES

*This quilt features two different setting triangles. The four at the top and bottom of the quilt include a Nine-Patch unit, while the six on the sides include a green square.*

## Setting Triangle A

1. Using the 16—1⅞" dark green leaf print (I) squares, 4—1⅞" green/gold floral (L) squares, and 16—1⅞" light tan plume print (E) squares, create a total of four Nine-Patch units.

2. Sew a 4⅞" light green background print (N) triangle to each side of a Nine-Patch unit.

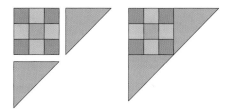

3. Sew the unit from step 1 to the top of a light green background print (N) parallellogram.

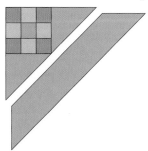

4. Repeat steps 2 and 3 to create a total of four Setting Triangle As.

## SETTING TRIANGLE B

Using the 6—4½" dark green floral (M) squares, 12 light green background print (N) triangles, and six light green background print (N) parallelograms, create a total of six Setting Triangle Bs.

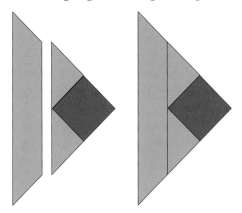

## QUILT CENTER

1. Referring to the quilt assembly diagram on page 65, lay out the Block As, Bs, and Cs; the Setting Triangle As and Bs; and four corner triangles.

2. Referring to the quilt assembly diagram, sew the units from step 1 into diagonal rows, then join the rows to complete the quilt center.

## FIRST INNER BORDER

*This border blends into the quilt center since it uses the same fabric as the background print in the quilt center's setting triangles.*

1. Measure the quilt center from top to bottom through the center. Piece two 1½"-wide light green background print (N) strips end to end, then cut to match that measurement. Repeat to make a second inner border strip. Referring to the quilt assembly diagram, sew these two strips to the sides of the quilt center. Press the seams toward the inner border.

2. Measure the quilt top from side to side through the center (including the borders you just added). Piece two 1½"-wide light green background print (N) strips end to end, then cut to match that measurement. Repeat to make a second inner border strip. Referring to the quilt assembly diagram, sew these two strips to the top and bottom of the quilt top. Press the seams toward the inner border.

## SECOND INNER BORDER

1. Measure the quilt top from top to bottom through the center. Piece two 2¾"-wide dark green print 1 (D) strips end to end, then cut to match that measurement. Repeat to make a second inner border strip. Referring to the quilt assembly diagram, sew these two strips to the sides of the quilt top. Press the seams toward the inner border.

2. Measure the quilt top from side to side through the center (including the borders you just added). Piece two 2¾"-wide dark green print 1 (D) strips end to end, then cut to match that measurement. Repeat to make a second inner border strip. Referring to the quilt assembly diagram, sew these two strips to the top and bottom of the quilt top. Press the seams toward the inner border.

## OUTER BORDER

*The outer border features on-point Nine-Patch units in the top left and lower right corners.*

1. Using the 5—1⅞" green/gold floral (L) squares and 4—1⅞" light green vine (O) squares, make a Nine-Patch unit. Repeat to make a total of 14 Nine-Patch units.

2. Referring to the following diagram, sew a dark green print 2 (P) triangle to opposite sides of a Nine-Patch unit from step 1. Repeat to make a total of six of these units.

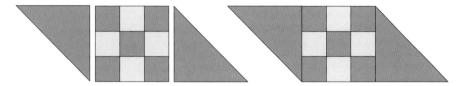

3. Referring to the following diagram, sew together a Nine-Patch unit from step 1, two small dark green print 2 (P) triangles, and a larger dark green print 2 (P) triangle. Repeat to make a total of eight of these units.

4. Sew a unit from step 3 to both ends of a unit from step 2. Repeat to make a second unit.

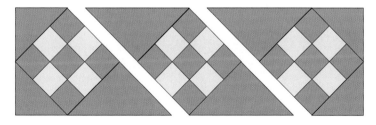

5. Sew together two units from step 2, then sew a unit from step 3 to both ends of it. Repeat to make a second unit.

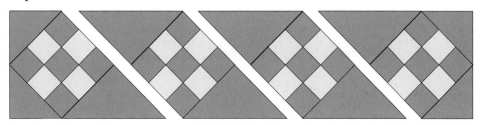

6. Measure the quilt top from top to bottom through the center. Measure the length of a unit from step 4, then subtract that measurement from the length of the quilt top and add ½" to that measurement to account for seam allowances. Piece two 6½"-wide dark green print 2 (P) print strips end to end, then cut to match that measurement. Sew this strip to a unit from step 4. Repeat to create a second strip. Referring to the quilt assembly diagram, sew these two strips to opposite sides of the quilt top.

7. Measure the quilt top from side to side through the center (including the borders you just added). Measure the length of a unit from step 5, then subtract that measurement from the width of the quilt top and add ½" to that measurement to account for seam allowances. Piece two 6½"-wide green print 2 (P) strips end to end, then cut to match that measurement. Sew this strip to a unit from step 5. Repeat to create a second strip. Referring to the quilt assembly diagram, sew these two strips to the top and bottom of the quilt top.

8. Sandwich the quilt top, batting, and backing; baste. Quilt as desired, then bind.

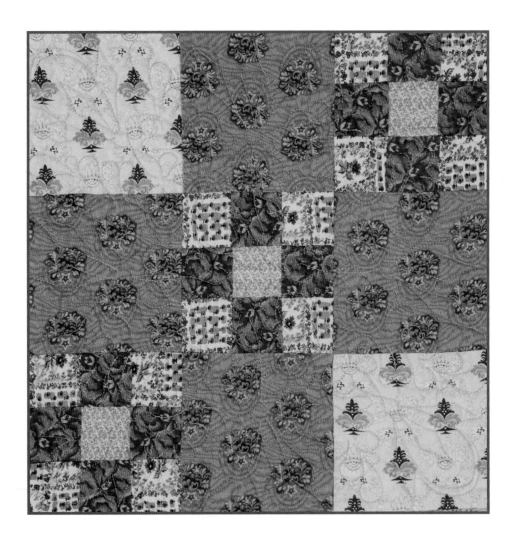

Assembly Diagram

# CORNELIA HANCOCK

Cornelia Hancock was motivated to serve during the Civil War after watching her brother and cousins march off to fight against the South. Her first efforts at volunteering were rejected by Dorothea Dix because she was too young, at age 21, and too pretty. During the Battle of Gettysburg in 1863, Hancock's brother-in-law, an Army doctor, asked her to come and help tend to wounded soldiers. More than 15,000 wounded men were left on the battlefield following this extended battle, and as the Union soldiers left to pursue Confederate forces, the doctors simply needed every available body to help. Hancock wrote extensively about what she observed following that horrific battle. One of her first letters on July 7, 1863, noted:

> I was the first woman who reached the Second Corps after the three days fight of Gettysburg. I was in that corps all day, not another woman within ½ mile . . . women are needed very badly. There are no words in the English language to express the suffering I witnessed today. The men lie on the ground; their clothes have been cut off them to dress their wounds. They are half naked, have nothing but hard tack [very dense crackers] to eat only as the Sanitary Commissions, Christian Association, and so forth give them.

> I gave to every man that had a leg or arm off a gill of wine, to every wounded in Third Division, one glass of lemonade, some bread and preserves and tobacco. They need it very much, they are so exhausted. I would get on first rate if they would not ask me to write to their wives; that I cannot do without crying.

The next day she wrote to her sister further describing what she observed. She cared for Union and Confederate soldiers alike.

> My Dear Sister,
> . . . I feel assured I shall never feel horrified at anything that may happen to me hereafter. There is a great want of surgeons here; there are hundreds of brave fellows, who have not had their wounds dressed since the battle. Brave is not the word; more, more Christian fortitude never was witnessed than they exhibit, always say "Help my neighbor first he is worse."

> I do not know when I shall go home-it will be according to how long this hospital stays here and whether another battle comes soon . . . It took nearly five days for some three hundred surgeons to perform the amputations that occurred here, during which time the rebels lay in a dying condition without their wounds being dressed or scarcely any food. If the rebels did not get severely punished for this battle, then I am no judge. We have but one rebel in our camp now; he says he never fired his gun if he could help it, and, therefore, we treat him first rate. One man died this morning. I fixed him up as nicely as the place will allow; he will be buried this afternoon. We are becoming somewhat civilized here now and the men are cared for well.

Following her work at Gettysburg, Hancock made her way to Washington, D.C., where she soon focused on the plight of freed slaves. As more and more former slaves journeyed north, Washington was soon overwhelmed and unable to adequately shelter or feed all of the people. On November 5, 1863, Cornelia wrote:

> I shall depict our wants in true but ardent words, hoping to affect you to some action. Here are gathered the sick from the contraband camps in the northern part of Washington. If I were to describe this hospital it would not be believed. North of Washington, in an open, muddy mire, are gathered all the colored people who have been made free by the progress of our Army. Sickness is inevitable, and to meet it these rude hospitals, only rough wooden barracks, are in use-a place where there is so much to be done you need not remain idle. We average here one birth per day, and have no baby clothes except as we wrap them up in an old piece of muslin, that even being scarce. Now the Army is advancing it is not uncommon to see from 40 to 50 arrivals in one day. They go at first to the Camp but many of them being sick from exhaustion soon come to us. They have nothing that any one, in the North would call clothing. I always see them as soon as they arrive, as they come here to be vaccinated; about 25 a day are vaccinated. This hospital is the reservoir for all cripples, diseased, aged, wounded, infirm, from whatsoever cause; all accidents happening to colored people in all employs around Washington are brought here. It is not uncommon for a colored driver to be pounded nearly to death by some of the white soldiers. We had a dreadful case of Hernia brought in today. A woman was brought here with three children by her side; said she had been on the road for some time; a more forlorn, worn out looking creature I never beheld. Her four eldest children are still in Slavery, her husband is dead. When I first saw her she laid on the floor, leaning against a bed, her children crying around her. One child died almost immediately, the other two are still sick. She seemed to need most, food and rest, and those two comforts we gave her, but clothes she still wants . . .

Hancock was eventually asked to return to the front lines of the battlefield, and she traveled extensively for more than a year, often following General Ulysses S. Grant, who she also wrote about:

> The idea of making a business of maiming men is not worthy of a civilization. I do not see Grant has accomplished much, yet he fights right straight ahead whether he gets any advantage or not.

Eventually, Hancock settled at a hospital in City Point, Virginia, which had room for up to 10,000 patients. She continued working there until the end of the war. Throughout her nursing work, she never forgot about the poor conditions experienced by emancipated slaves. Following the end of the war, Hancock opened a school for former slaves in South Carolina and taught there herself for ten years. She then relocated to Philadelphia where she founded the Children's Aid Society in 1878. She remained an active force in several charities until age 74 when she finally retired from her various activities and moved to Atlantic City to live with family. She died at the age of 87.

# The BLUE and the GRAY

*Designed and made by Dolores Smith*

Finished quilt size: 71" x 79"
Finished block size: 8" x 8"

This quilt features a single block design, but reversing the light and dark prints within it creates an intriguing interplay of pattern. For a scrappy look, I combined several different blue and gray reproduction prints.

## Fabric Requirements

+ 3 yards total or 12 fat quarters shirtings for blocks
+ 3 yards total or 12 fat quarters gray and blue prints for blocks
+ ¾ yard tan print for inner border
+ 2½ yards dark blue print for outer border and binding

## Cutting Instructions

*Block cutting instructions below are for one block only.*

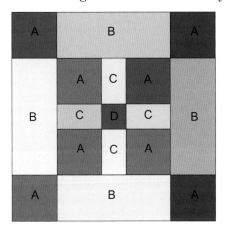
**BLOCK A**

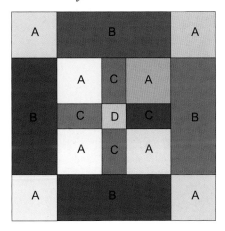
**BLOCK B**

### From assorted blue and gray prints, cut:
• 8—2¼" squares (A) for Block A
• 4—2¼" x 5" rectangles (B) for Block B
• 4—1⅜" x 2¼" rectangles (C) for Block B
• 1—1⅜" square (D) for Block A

### From assorted shirtings, cut:
• 8—2¼" squares (A) for Block B
• 4—2¼" x 5" rectangles (B) for Block A
• 4—1⅜" x 2¼" rectangles (C) for Block A
• 1—1⅜" square (D) for Block B

### From tan print, cut:
• 8—2" strips the width of fabric for inner border

### From blue print, cut:
• 8—6½" strips the width of fabric for outer border
• 8—2½" strips the width of fabric for binding

## BLOCK A

1. Referring to the following diagram, sew together 4—2¼" (A) blue and gray squares, 4—1⅜" x 2¼" (C) shirting rectangles, and 1—1⅜" blue or gray (D) square.

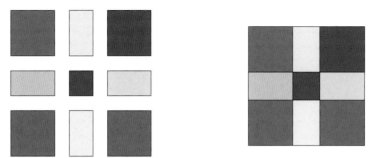

2. Sew a 2¼" x 5" (B) shirting rectangle to opposite sides of the unit from step 1.

3. Sew a 2¼" blue or gray (A) square to both ends of a 2¼" x 5" (B) shirting rectangle. Repeat to make two of these units, then sew these units to the top and bottom of the unit from step 2.

4. Repeat steps 1–3 to make a total of 28 Block As.

## BLOCK B

Reverse the placement of the shirtings and the blue/gray prints to create a total of 28 Block Bs.

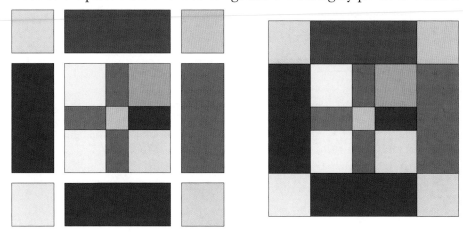

# Quilt Assembly

1. Referring to the photo of the quilt on page 68 for placement, sew a row of seven blocks, starting with a Block B and alternating with a Block A. Repeat to make a total of four of these rows.

2. Referring to the photo of the quilt on page 68 for placement, sew a row of seven blocks, starting with a Block A and alternating with a Block B. Repeat to make a total of four of these rows.

3. Referring to the quilt assembly diagram on page 72, lay out the rows from steps 1 and 2, starting with a row from step 1 and alternating with a row from step 2.

4. Join the rows to create the quilt center, which should measure 56½" x 64½".

5. Measure the quilt center from top to bottom through the center. Piece two 2"-wide tan print strips end to end, then cut to match that measurement. Repeat to make a second inner border strip. Referring to the quilt assembly diagram, sew these two strips to the sides of the quilt center. Press the seams toward the inner border.

6. Measure the quilt top from side to side through the center (including the borders you just added). Piece two 2"-wide tan print strips end to end, then cut to match that measurement. Repeat to make a second inner border strip. Referring to the quilt assembly diagram, sew these two strips to the top and bottom of the quilt top. Press the seams toward the inner border.

7. Measure the quilt top from top to bottom through the center. Piece two 6½"-wide blue print strips end to end, then cut to match that measurement. Repeat to make a second outer border strip. Referring to the quilt assembly diagram, sew these two strips to the sides of the quilt top. Press the seams toward the outer border.

8. Measure the quilt top from side to side through the center (including the borders you just added). Piece two 6½"-wide blue print strips end to end, then cut to match that measurement. Repeat to make a second outer border strip. Referring to the quilt assembly diagram, sew these two strips to the top and bottom of the quilt top. Press the seams toward the outer border.

9. Sandwich the quilt top, batting, and backing; baste. Quilt as desired, then bind.

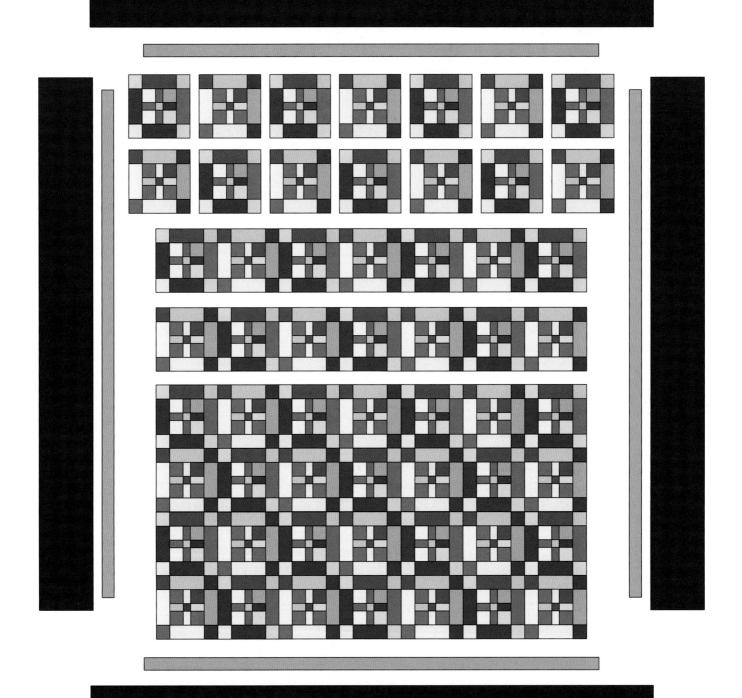

*Assembly Diagram*

# MARY PHINNEY

Many women of high social status responded to the call for service during the Civil War. One of them was Mary Phinney, whose marriage to a German baron made her Baroness Gustav von Olnhausen. Phinney worked at the Mansion House Hospital in Alexandria, Virginia. Like some of her fellow nurses, Phinney maintained written records that described wartime conditions. In this entry from March 1863, she recounts what she found when she arrived at the hospital:

Miss Dix, who had been appointed by the President head of the army nurses, took me from Washington to Alexandria to the Mansion House Hospital. She told me on the journey that the surgeon in charge was determined to give her no foothold in any hospital where he reigned, and that I was to take no notice of anything that might occur, and was to make no complaint whatever might happen. She was a stern woman of few words.

There seemed to be much confusion about the Mansion House-which before the war was a famous hotel-and every part of it was crowded. She left me in the office and went in search of Dr. S. The sight of the wounded continuously carried through on stretchers, or led in as they arrived from the boats that lay at the foot of the street on which the hospital stood (this was just after that awful Cedar Mountain battle [August 1862]), seemed more than I could bear, and I thought Miss Dix would never come. At last she appeared, with Dr. S., who eyed me keenly and, it seemed to me, very savagely, and gave me in charge of an orderly to show me to the surgical ward, as it was called. It consisted of many small rooms, with a broad corridor, every room so full of cots that it was only barely possible to pass between them. Such a sorrowful sight; the men had just been taken off the battle-field, some of them had been lying three or four days almost without clothing, their wounds never dressed, so dirty and wretched. Someone gave me my charges as to what I was to do; it seemed such a hopeless task to do anything to help them that I wanted to throw myself down and give it up. Miss Dix left me, and soon the doctors came and ordered me to follow them while they examined and dressed the wounds. They seemed to me then, and afterwards I found they were, the most brutal men I ever saw.

So I began my work, I might say night and day. The surgeon told me he had no room for me, and a nurse told me he said he would make the house so hot for me I would not stay long. When I told Miss Dix I could not remain without a room to sleep in, she, knowing the plan of driving me out, said,

"My child" (I was nearly as old as herself), "you will stay where I have placed you." In the meantime McClellan's army was being landed below us from the Peninsula. Night and day the rumbling of heavy cannon, the marching of soldiers, the groaning of the sick and wounded were constantly heard; and yet in all that time I never once looked from the windows, I was so busy with the men.

One of the rooms of the ward was the operating-room, and the passing in and out of those who were to be operated upon, and the coming and going of the surgeons added so much to the general confusion. I doubt if at any time during the war there was ever such confusion as at this time. The insufficient help, the unskillful surgeons, and a general want of organization were very distressing; but I was too busy then and too tired for want of proper sleep to half realize it. Though I slept at the bedsides of the men or in a corner of the rooms, I was afraid to complain lest I be discharged. I was horribly ignorant, of course, and could only try to make the men comfortable; but the staff doctors were very friendly and occasionally helped me, and someone occasionally showed me about bandaging, so by degrees I began to do better. The worst doctor had been discharged, much to my joy, but the other one, despite his drinking habits, stayed on. After the morning visit it was no use calling upon him for anything, and I had to rely on the officer of the day if I needed help. I know now that many a life could have been saved if there had been a competent surgeon in the ward.

At this time the ward was full of very sick men and sometimes two would be dying at the same time, and both begging me to stay with them, so I got little sleep or rest. Moreover, I had no room of my own. Occasionally a nurse would extend the hospitality of the floor in hers, and I would have a straw bed dragged in on which to get a few hours' sleep. This, with a hurried bath and fresh clothes, was my only rest for weeks. It was no use to complain. The surgeon simply stormed at me and said there was no room, while Miss Dix would say, "You can bear it awhile, my child; I have placed you here and you must stay." I was at that time her only nurse in the Mansion House. Later she succeeded in getting rid of all the others and replacing them with her own.

Despite her experiences, Phinney came to enjoy nursing. Following the war, she traveled in Europe for a while. When she returned to the United States, she resumed her nursing career.

# OLD GLORY

*Designed and made by Dolores Smith*

Finished size: 16" x 54"

This fun, fast project can easily be completed in a day. Want a smaller version? Simply shorten the stripes and stripe background, and reduce the size of the star and star background.

## Fabric Requirements

*Dolores used felted hand-dyed wool for her pillow.*

+ 17" x 55" white wool for pillow front background
+ 9" x 17" white wool for star
+ 10" x 25" blue wool for star background
+ 8½" x 55" red wool for stripes
+ 18" x 55" fabric of choice for backing (Dolores used a cotton ticking)
+ 2 bags polyester fiberfill or stuffing of your choice

## Cutting Instructions

**From white wool, cut:**
- 1 star from template on page 79 (Dolores traced the star template onto freezer paper with a black marker or pencil, then pressed the shiny side of the freezer paper down onto the white wool before cutting out the star shape. Be sure to remove the freezer paper before you appliqué the star in place.)
- 1—14½" x 55" strip for pillow front background

**From red wool, cut:**
- 3—2½" x 55" strips for stripes

**From blue wool, cut:**
- 1—8½" x 24" rectangle for star background

## Sewing Instructions

1. Referring to the appliqué placement diagram on page 80, lay out the three red stripes on the 14½" x 55" white background, then the blue star background in the upper left-hand corner. When you are satisfied with their placement, pin the star to the blue star background, then the red stripes and the blue star background to the pillow top background.

2. Using a running stitch, appliqué the red stripes, then the blue star background to the pillow top.

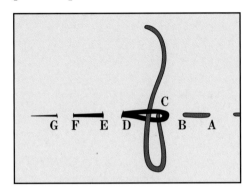

**RUNNING STITCH**

3. Using a whipstitch, appliqué the star on top of the blue wool background rectangle.

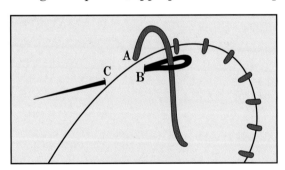

**WHIPSTITCH**

4. Measure the pillow top, then cut the pillow back the same size. With right sides together, pin the pillow back to the pillow top.

5. Using a ½" seam allowance, sew around the pillow perimeter, leaving an 8" opening at the bottom for stuffing the pillow. Trim the corners for turning.

6. Turn the pillow right side out, then stuff it with polyester fiberfill or your choice of stuffing.

7. Using a whipstitch, sew the opening shut.